ECO-ACTION

Buildings
of the Future

Angela Royston

Heinemann Library
Chicago, Illinois

© 2008 Heinemann Library
a division of Reed Elsevier Inc.
Chicago, Illinois

Customer Service 888-454-2279
Visit our website at www.heinemannlibrary.com

Designed by Philippa Jenkins and Michelle
    Lisseter
Illustrations by Nicholas Beresford-Davies p. 8;
    Bridge Creative Services p. 6; Jeff Edwards p. 43;
    Philippa Jenkins p. 10; Gary Slater pp. 15, 19,
    25; David Woodroffe p. 9
Printed and bound in China by South China
    Printing Co. Ltd.

12 11 10 09 08
10 9 8 7 6 5 4 3 2 1

**Library of Congress Cataloging-in-Publication
Data**
Royston, Angela.
    Buildings of the future / Angela Royston.
        p. cm. -- (Eco-action)
Includes bibliographical references and index.
ISBN 978-1-4329-0126-4 (library binding :
hardcover) -- ISBN 978-1-4329-0131-8 (pbk.)
1. Sustainable buildings--Juvenile literature.
2. Buildings--Energy conservation--Juvenile
literature. 3. Buildings--Environmental aspects--
Juvenile literature. 4. Carbon dioxide mitigation-
-Juvenile literature. 5. Global warming--
Prevention--Juvenile literature.
I. Title.
TH880.R69 2007
720'.47--dc22
                                    2007005804

Acknowledgments
The publishers would like to thank the following
for permission to reproduce photographs:
©Alamy pp. **21** (Andrew Butterton), **39**
(GardenWorld Images), **35** (Ian Leonard), **19** (Paul
Glendell), **20** (Realimage), **41** (Sindre Ellingsen),
29 (Skyscan Photolibrary), **24** (Wolfgang Kaehler);
©Corbis pp. **16** (Bob Sacha), **26** (epa/Shawn
Thew), **12** (James Leynse), **7** (Paul Souders),
37 (Reuters/Jason Reed), **30** (zefa/C. Lyttle);
©Empics p. **5** lower (AP Photo/Jose Luis
Magana); ©Illinois Department of Commerce
and Community Affairs p. **5** top (Mike
Gustafson); ©istockphoto.com pp. **11**, **14**
(Charles Humphries), **38** (Diane Diederich), **33**
(Jim Jurica), **36** (John Chiembanchong), **34** (Ray
Haciosmanoglu); ©Panos Pictures pp. **40** (Fred
Hoogervorst); ©PhotoEdit, Inc. p. **17** (Ulrike
Welsh); ©Science Photo Library p. **32** (Tony
McConnell); ©Steve Thomas from Monodraught
Ltd p. **18**; ©Still Pictures pp. **27** top and bottom
(Bruce Molnia), p. **42**, **29** top (Mark Edwards),
23 (Martin Bond), **13** (Oldrich Karasek).

Cover photograph of Seattle office building,
reproduced with permission of Masterfile/
Mike Dobel.

Disclaimer
All the Internet addresses (URLs) given in this
book were valid at time of going to press.
However, due to the dynamic nature of the
Internet, some addresses may have changed, or
sites may have changed or ceased to exist since
publication. While the author and publishers
regret any inconvenience this may cause readers,
no responsibility for any such changes can be
accepted by either the author or the publishers.
It is recommended that adults supervise children
on the Internet.

Contents

Any words appearing in the text in bold, **like this**, are explained in the Glossary.

The Big Challenge

There is a problem facing the world that is bigger than any other problem. It is even bigger than disease, war, or crime. The greatest problem is **climate change** caused by **global warming**. Earth is becoming warmer. In the last 150 years, the average worldwide temperature has increased by 1.4 °Fahrenheit (0.8 °Celsius), with most of this increase occurring in the last 50 years. This may not sound like much, but, if it is allowed to continue, Earth could warm by a further 9 °F (5 °C) by the year 2100.

Global catastrophes

Global warming disrupts the weather and causes catastrophes such as **droughts**, famines, and disease. As the temperature rises, polar ice begins to melt, causing **sea levels** to rise and low-lying coasts to flood. If this continues unchecked, some cities, including New York and London, will be flooded, as will huge areas of low-lying land in countries such as Belgium and Bangladesh.

What do buildings have to do with global warming?

Buildings contribute to global warming because they use energy produced by burning coal, oil, and natural gas. Buildings use huge amounts of energy, particularly electricity. Electricity powers air conditioning, lighting, and all the machines that homes, schools, offices, factories, and other buildings use. The materials that buildings are made of are manufactured using energy, too. Architects and engineers are devising different ways of building that will use less energy in the future. They are also finding ways of supplying buildings with energy that do not contribute to global warming.

Existing buildings

Buildings are usually built to last a long time. Some buildings today, such as churches and government centers, were built hundreds of years ago.

Modern buildings, such as these skyscrapers in Chicago, use a lot of energy. They are eye-catching and impressive, but they are adding to the problem of global warming.

Rather than knock all these buildings down and build new ones, people have to find ways of adapting them so that these buildings stop adding to global warming.

Building for the future

As the world's climate changes, there will be more severe weather—more **hurricanes** and **typhoons**, more heat waves, and more droughts. Architects need to design buildings in the future so that they can withstand extreme weather. This book looks at the challenge that is facing architects and builders—how to design buildings that will cut the increase in global warming and will survive climate change. But first we have to look more closely at global warming and what causes it.

Global warming will cause more natural disasters, such as this flood in Mexico.

Global Warming

Heat from the Sun passes through the atmosphere and warms the surface of Earth. Some of the heat is reflected back into the air, but most is absorbed by the land and sea and then released into the atmosphere. Global warming is occurring because less heat is escaping into space. It is being trapped in the atmosphere instead.

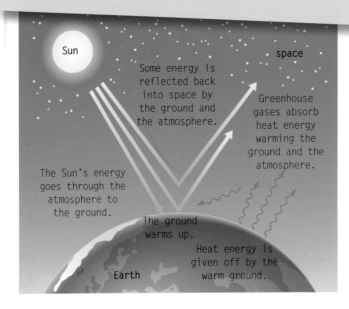

Sun

space

Some energy is reflected back into space by the ground and the atmosphere.

Greenhouse gases absorb heat energy warming the ground and the atmosphere.

The Sun's energy goes through the atmosphere to the ground.

The ground warms up.

Heat energy is given off by the warm ground.

Earth

Greenhouse gases and clouds absorb some of the Sun's heat, making Earth warmer than it would otherwise be.

Greenhouse effect

Clouds, which are made of water vapor and water droplets, absorb some of the heat from Earth's surface, and so do **carbon dioxide** and certain other gases. They are called **greenhouse gases** because they trap the heat, and warm Earth, just as a greenhouse warms the air inside it. During the last century, more and more greenhouse gases have built up in the atmosphere, making Earth increasingly warm.

Effects of global warming

Scientists use computers to predict what will happen as the air heats up. The most damaging change has already started in Earth's coldest places—the Arctic and the Antarctic. Here, rising temperatures are melting the **glaciers**, which are slow-moving sheets of thick ice.

As they melt, extra water flows into the oceans—so much water that the sea level is slowly rising. Eventually it will flood low-lying land around the coast. Half of the world's people live on or near the coast, so many villages, towns, and cities could disappear beneath the sea.

Storms, drought, and disease

Even before coasts are flooded, global warming will disrupt the world's climates. Severe storms, which have become more common since 1990, will increase, and more places will suffer from long droughts. Deserts, which are already spreading, will spread faster.

Some places will be wetter, and many parts of North America and Europe will be much warmer. So warm, in fact, that malarial **mosquitoes** will thrive in countries that are currently too cold for them. These mosquitoes will infect millions more people with **malaria**, a potentially fatal disease. At the same time, scientists think that ocean currents could change. These ocean currents bring large amounts of heat. Without this heat, the average temperatures in parts of eastern North America and in Europe could drop significantly.

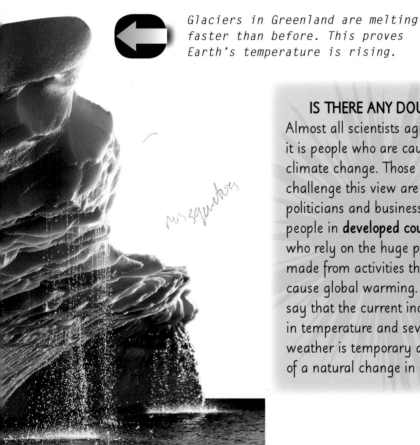

Glaciers in Greenland are melting faster than before. This proves Earth's temperature is rising.

IS THERE ANY DOUBT?
Almost all scientists agree that it is people who are causing climate change. Those who challenge this view are mainly politicians and business people in **developed countries** who rely on the huge profits made from activities that cause global warming. They say that the current increase in temperature and severe weather is temporary and part of a natural change in climate.

Carbon dioxide is the most abundant of the damaging greenhouse gases. Carbon dioxide is produced all the time by all living things—including plants, animals, and people—but the carbon dioxide emitted by living things is balanced by the amount of carbon dioxide plants take in. So, living things do not add to the amount of carbon dioxide in the atmosphere. Global warming is mainly caused by the extra carbon dioxide produced from burning **fossil fuels**.

Carbon cycle

Plants absorb carbon dioxide from the air to make a sugary food that contains carbon. The process is called **photosynthesis**. Animals depend on plants for food, either because they eat plants or because they eat animals that eat plants. Living things need food to survive and to grow. As their bodies burn the energy in food, they produce waste carbon dioxide, which is breathed out. When plants and animals die, their bodies usually rot, producing carbon dioxide. Carbon passes through living things in a continuous cycle called the **carbon cycle**.

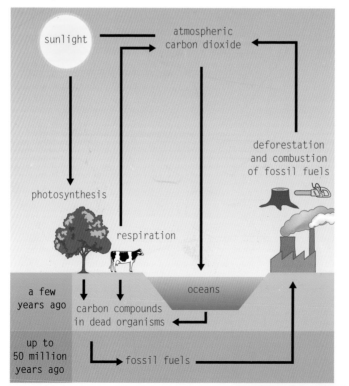

About the same amount of carbon dioxide produced by living things is absorbed and recycled by plants during photosynthesis.

Fossil fuels

In the past—about 300 million years ago, before dinosaurs roamed Earth—huge quantities of trees and other plants in forests died and were buried before they could rot. Silt and other sediments accumulated on top of them and slowly compressed them. The layers of silt and sediment gradually became rocks, and the remains of the plants between the rocks changed into coal and natural gas. In a similar way, the remains of billions of tiny sea creatures that lived even earlier formed oil and natural gas. Coal, oil, and gas are called fossil fuels.

Instead of the remains rotting and producing carbon dioxide, the carbon was locked into the fossil fuel. Because coal, oil, and gas contain carbon, they make good fuels. But when they are burned, they produce carbon dioxide and other greenhouse gases. In the last 100 years, people have been burning more fossil fuels, which produce most of the extra greenhouses gases.

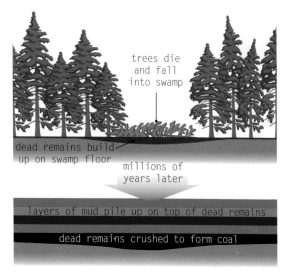

trees die and fall into swamp

dead remains build up on swamp floor

millions of years later

layers of mud pile up on top of dead remains

dead remains crushed to form coal

Coal and natural gas formed very slowly over millions of years. When we have used up our supplies, there will be no more.

SUPPLIES OF FOSSIL FUELS

There is still plenty of coal in the ground, but we should mine as little of it as possible because coal is the most polluting fossil fuel. It not only produces greenhouses gases, it also creates other particles that hang in the air. Oil and gas are found deep under the ground or under the seabed. People only started drilling for oil about 1 00 years ago, but we have now used so much that supplies are becoming more difficult to find. However, we still have large stocks of natural gas. This is good news because natural gas creates less carbon dioxide than other fossil fuels.

How buildings contribute to global warming

Buildings, transportation, industry, and **power stations** all rely on burning fossil fuels to get energy. Natural gas and oil are used for heating. Coal, oil, and natural gas are used to generate electricity, much of which is used in buildings. Oil is mainly made into gasoline, diesel, and aircraft fuel to drive our machines and vehicles. Some of these machines, such as bulldozers, backhoes, cranes, and cement mixers, are used to construct new buildings, while trucks carry building materials from **quarries** and factories to building sites.

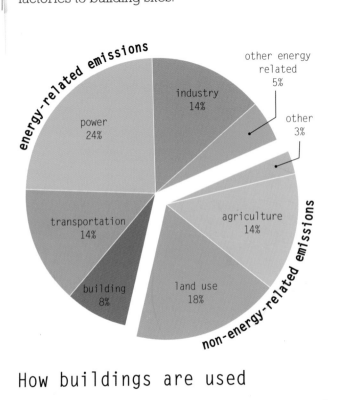

energy-related emissions

other energy
related
5%

industry
14%

power
24%

other
3%

transportation
14%

agriculture
14%

building
8%

land use
18%

non-energy-related emissions

Buildings create 8 percent of carbon dioxide by burning fossil fuels like coal and oil for heating. Buildings, however, also consume most of the electricity generated by power stations, so overall they are responsible for about one-third of carbon dioxide **emissions.**

How buildings are used

Buildings provide us with shelter. They protect us from rain, wind, heat, and cold. We have different buildings for different purposes, so that in a single day you may leave your home, go to a school, and visit a store, library, or stadium. Your parents may work in an office, factory, or hospital. All of these buildings are heated and cooled, depending on the temperature outside. In the past, people would heat only one or two rooms in winter, and almost no one had air conditioning in the summer. Although central heating, air conditioning, and a range of electrical machines have made living and working in buildings more comfortable and convenient, the energy they use produces billions of tons of carbon dioxide.

Large buildings

Large modern buildings are usually many stories high. Skyscrapers now dominate most city skylines. They are designed to look spectacular and impressive and, as cities become larger and more crowded, they have the advantage of fitting many people into a small area of ground. Most large modern buildings are made of concrete, steel, and glass. Their windows seldom open, so the air inside has to be air conditioned. Glass lets in sunlight, but it also lets in the Sun's heat—although a new type of glass now keeps out the Sun's heat. Nevertheless, older offices can become unbearably hot in summer, so air conditioning has to use even more energy to make the building cool enough to work in.

Changing the way we live

To slow down global warming, we have to stop burning so much fossil fuel. Architects, engineers, and scientists have to find new ways of designing and constructing buildings so that they produce little or no carbon dioxide. The good news is that architects have already built experimental homes that produce no carbon dioxide. New technology is already being used that leads the way to the buildings of the future.

People in offices waste huge amounts of energy by, for example, leaving lights and computers on all night.

Buildings of the Future

Buildings account for about one-third of all carbon dioxide emissions, so it is essential that buildings in the future rely much less on fossil fuels. They can do this in two ways—by using less energy, particularly for heating and air conditioning, and by using electricity generated from **renewable** sources. A renewable source of energy, such as the Sun or the wind, is one that will not run out and that creates no carbon dioxide.

Lost energy

At present most buildings use electricity that is generated in power stations, and much of the energy is lost in the process. In many countries and in parts of the United States, Canada, and Australia, the electricity is transmitted along cables in a huge network or grid. More energy is then lost in the transmission. In the future much of the energy will be generated within each building or locally.

This house in New Jersey uses 80 percent less energy than an average U.S. home. Its solar-powered water heating system, compact flourescent lightbulbs, and concrete walls all help it to save energy.

Building to fit the climate

Climates will become more extreme as global warming progresses. Hot countries will become hotter, and many countries will become drier. Some may even become colder. It is important that buildings are designed to suit the climate. In cooler countries, well-designed buildings can gain free heat from the Sun, but buildings in hot countries need to be protected from the Sun. Good design means that the buildings use less energy for heating and air conditioning.

*Mongolia is a cold, desert country to the north of China. **Nomads** there traditionally live in yurts. The thick covering is windproof as well as waterproof, and all the heat comes from a single stove in the middle of the tent.*

TRADITIONAL SHAPES

People have long survived in the coldest of climates using very simple building methods. The most spectacular example is the Inuit, who built shelters made of snow. The round shape of an **igloo**, like the round shape of a Mongolian **yurt**, is ideal for resisting wind and reducing the amount of warmth lost through the walls. In hot countries, people have found many different ways to keep their homes cool (see page 18).

Rediscovering traditional ways

Building to suit the climate is not a new idea. Traditional ways of building often do just that, but modern ways of building—using heavy machines, concrete, and steel frames—broke away from traditional methods and very often lost their advantages. This is not to say that we must simply go back to traditional forms of building, but we can learn from them how to design buildings in the future that take the climate into account and therefore use less energy.

Using the Sun

The Sun beams down huge amounts of energy every day. In cool, temperate countries, buildings should be designed and positioned to make use of as much of the Sun's energy as possible. At present, heating and cooling a building consumes huge amounts of energy. In tropical countries, and in countries with hot summers, buildings should be designed to shade the rooms from the hot Sun.

Passive solar heating

Using the heat of the Sun to heat a building is called **passive solar heating** because once the building is in place, no more needs to be done about it and the heating costs nothing! In the northern hemisphere, the south-facing sides of a building get the most sunshine. In cooler countries, therefore, these are the sides of the building that should have the most window space. Windows high up a wall take heat and light deeper inside the building. During the day a sun porch or greenhouse can trap the Sun's heat and warm the air before it passes into the rest of the house.

Keeping out the sunshine

In hot countries, people want to escape the Sun's heat, particularly in the middle of the day. Stone, bricks, and tiles made from clay or mud absorb heat and warm up slowly. They are good materials for walls and floors because, as the temperature cools at night, they slowly release their stored heat.

Traditional homes in hot countries have shutters and a shady veranda or courtyard to keep them cool. Shaded balconies could work just as well on tall buildings.

Solar pipes

Solar pipes work like a **skylight**, only better. They are particularly good for modern buildings with dark rooms or hallways that are usually lit all day by electric lights. Skylights let in only a straight beam of light, but solar pipes bend the light and take it deeper into the building. Although they are expensive to buy, they cost nothing once installed and use no energy.

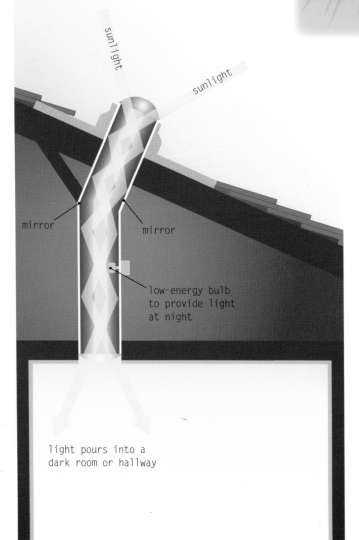

sunlight

sunlight

mirror

mirror

low-energy bulb
to provide light
at night

light pours into a
dark room or hallway

SHUTTERS OR BLINDS
Pulling down a blind or drawing a curtain inside a window does not cut out all of the Sun's heat. And, once the Sun's heat has passed through the glass, it cannot escape. Shutters that can be closed outside the window during the heat of the day keep a room much cooler.

A solar pipe takes sunlight into darker areas inside a building. The inside of the tube is lined with mirrors to make the light brighter even on cloudy days.

Solar panels

There are two kinds of **solar panels**—solar collectors that heat water and **photovoltaic panels** (called PV panels for short) that generate electricity. Both kinds work best in countries that get plenty of hot sunshine, but they also work in cooler, cloudier countries, such as Japan, Canada, and Germany.

Heating water

Many buildings in hot countries, such as Greece, already have solar panels that heat the water. The Sun's heat passes through the surface of the panel and heats water in narrow pipes below. Within the United States, solar water heating could provide two-thirds of all the hot water that buildings need. The disadvantage of solar energy is that there is, of course, no sunshine at night. If the heated water is stored in a well-insulated tank, however, it can give a constant supply.

Solar panels are put on roofs at an angle to catch more sunshine.

Photovoltaic panels

PV panels were developed to generate electricity on spacecraft. Now, the same space-age technology is one of our best weapons in the fight against global warming. Each PV cell contains a substance that creates electricity when sunlight hits it. Since PV cells can be made about the same size as a roof tile, they can easily replace the tiles on the sunny side of a sloping roof. Flat roofs need to have special arrays of solar cells, slanted to catch the most sunlight.

The United States and Japan are leading the way in developing PV cells, and many new buildings there use them to generate their own electricity. Many other countries have barely begun. Nevertheless, PV panels should soon be common on rooftops everywhere.

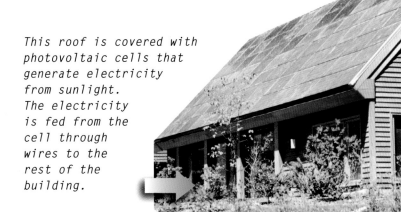

This roof is covered with photovoltaic cells that generate electricity from sunlight. The electricity is fed from the cell through wires to the rest of the building.

Advantages and disadvantages

Apart from generating electricity without creating greenhouse gases, PV cells can be installed on existing buildings as well as on new ones. This is a huge advantage, since relatively few buildings are built every year. Also, PV panels can sometimes generate more electricity than the building needs, in which case the excess electricity can be sold to the grid. Instead of costing money, the PV cells can make some money!

The main disadvantage of PV cells is that they are still very expensive to buy and install. Yet they are already much cheaper than they were 10 years ago, and they will become even cheaper as more people buy them and they are mass-produced. The other disadvantage is that they do not work at night. Unless electricity can be stored during the day, another source is needed at night.

Using the wind

The natural movement of air can be used to cool buildings and to ventilate them with fresh air. This saves the need for expensive air conditioning powered by electricity. In places that get strong winds, the power of the wind can be harnessed to generate electricity using **wind turbines**.

Air conditioning and ventilation

In the last 20 or 30 years, the amount of energy used for air conditioning has increased rapidly. Most large, modern buildings use it for ventilation, instead of opening windows to get fresh air. As the climate becomes warmer, the demand for air conditioning will grow to keep buildings cooler in summer. For air conditioning to work, the windows in a building have to be closed. In many modern buildings the windows are actually sealed shut. Yet with good design, the flow of fresh air can be used both to ventilate and to cool a building.

Countries that have had hot climates for a long time have traditionally used different ways to keep buildings cool. In North Africa, for example, buildings are often built around a central, shady courtyard. Most of the rooms open onto the courtyard, while the outer walls have few or no windows. Houses in Jamaica and Southeast Asia and traditional ranches in Australia are often built on stilts or on raised platforms. Cooler air is pulled through the house from below. In Yemen and other Arab countries, the buildings are tall, with windows near the top. This also pulls air through the house. Some of these ideas can be incorporated into modern buildings to cool them without using electricity.

BATTENING DOWN THE HATCHES

The wind can also be destructive. Severe storms will become more common everywhere, so buildings in the future will have to be built more strongly so that they can stand up to the force of a hurricane.

Windcatchers pull air down into a building to provide a draft of fresh air without using electricity.

Windcatchers and wind turbines

Windcatchers use the same idea as Middle Eastern wind towers. Windcatchers pull air down into the building to provide a draft of fresh air without using electricity. The wind, however, can also be used to generate electricity. In the past, people used windmills to grind corn. Modern wind turbines use rotating blades to generate electricity, and they work best where there is often a strong wind, along the coast or on hillsides. Although some people have installed wind turbines on their homes in towns and cities, they generate only a little electricity. Larger buildings, such as hospitals, supermarkets, and office blocks, can install bigger, free-standing turbines that generate much more electricity.

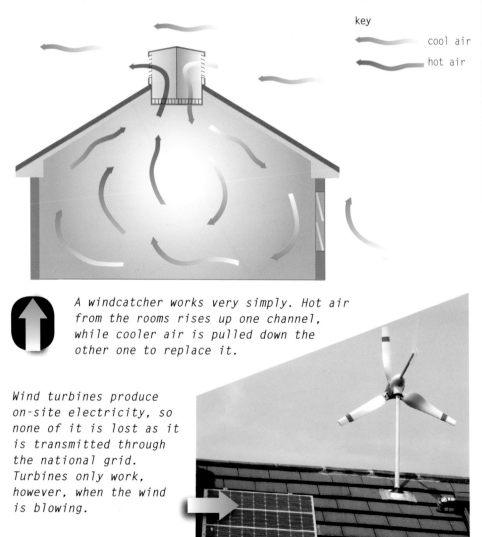

key

cool air

hot air

A windcatcher works very simply. Hot air from the rooms rises up one channel, while cooler air is pulled down the other one to replace it.

Wind turbines produce on-site electricity, so none of it is lost as it is transmitted through the national grid. Turbines only work, however, when the wind is blowing.

Building materials

Building materials use energy when they are manufactured and when they are transported to the building site. The best materials, therefore, are usually those that have been recycled and those that are found locally. Nevertheless, engineers have developed artificial materials that work very well in buildings, and environmentalists have been experimenting with alternative materials, such as **rammed earth**, which is similar to traditional mud bricks. Rammed earth is produced by compressing damp earth until it is very strong.

Insulating roofs

One of the best ways to reduce the amount of energy a building uses is to make sure that no energy is wasted. Insulating a roof stops heat from escaping in the winter and keeps the building cool in summer. In the past, people used to thatch roofs with straw, but today the insulating material is usually put on the inside. Glass fiber is an excellent **insulator**. It is a **synthetic material**, and so its manufacture creates carbon dioxide, but this is far outweighed by the carbon dioxide emissions it saves as an insulator.

Growing plants on a roof provides insulation.

GREEN ROOFS

One unusual way to insulate a flat roof is to create a garden on it. Many people have roof terraces with potted plants, but a **green roof** goes much further than that. The roof is covered with a layer of soil and planted with plants that do not need much care. The soil insulates the roof, keeping the house cool in summer as well as warm in winter, and the plants absorb carbon dioxide and rainwater.

This row of houses is part of the Beddington Zero Energy Development, known as BedZED. It was built in south London, United Kingdom, in 2002.

Insulating walls

Buildings lose heat through their roofs, windows, and walls, so new buildings need to be constructed using materials that cut out this loss. Many traditional materials, such as wood and mud, are good insulators, particularly in smaller buildings. Concrete is made by mixing sand, gravel, and cement. It is a very strong and versatile building material that can be molded into different shapes, but it takes a lot of energy to make and is not a particularly good insulator. Engineers, however, have developed foam concrete blocks, which are excellent insulators, for the inside of **cavity walls**.

ECO VILLAGE
In addition to 82 homes and work spaces for 100 people, BedZED has a health center, a nursery, an organic café, and sports facilities. The buildings face south to catch the most sunshine and are well insulated and triple glazed. As a consequence they use only 10 percent of the energy of traditional houses. The energy they use comes from solar panels and other renewable sources.

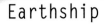

Earthship

U.S. architect Michael Reynolds has developed a carbon-free house called Earthship that can be built anywhere—in cities, in hot and cold countries, even in the Arizona desert. The house is constructed of recycled materials and rammed earth and is self-sufficient in energy. The people who live in an Earthship collect and recycle water and grow much or all of their food. It uses many of the techniques shown in the previous pages and a few more.

Building materials

Earthship is constructed of recycled materials—including timber, rubber tires, aluminium, and steel cans—and natural materials such as mud and sheep's wool. The tires are filled with rammed earth and made into bricks that are very strong. They are also good insulators. Wood is reclaimed from other buildings and used for floors and ceilings. The sheep's wool insulates the roof. Even recycled glass and cardboard is used in this extraordinary house.

Low energy

The house is situated to make the best use of the Sun. In cooler climates a large greenhouse is used to heat the air before it enters the rest of the building. Even in cold weather the inside feels warm, although there are no visible heaters. In summer and in hot climates, trees are used to shade the building from the Sun's heat.

Generating electricity

Earthship generates its own electricity using photovoltaic cells and a small wind turbine. The electricity is used mainly for lights, computers, and other electrical machines. Any excess is used to charge batteries, which can then be used at night and on dark, cloudy days. People who live in an Earthship are careful not to waste electricity and can store enough electricity in the batteries to last about 10 days.

Generating heat

Solar water-heating panels heat the water, and there is a wood stove for when extra heat is needed, either to heat the rooms or the water. The stove burns wood chips made from waste wood.

Water and waste

Rainwater supplies almost all the water the building needs. The water is collected and filtered so that it is safe to drink and to use for cooking. It is also recycled, so that waste water from washing dishes and clothes is used to water the plants.

Household waste is composted into soil to nourish the garden. Even sewage is recycled by turning it into compost. Other waste is recycled and used to build more Earthships!

This Earthsip was built from discarded vehicle tires, drink cans, and earth. It also uses passive solar heating (see page 14) and photovoltaic cells for generating electricity.

Other sources of energy

There are other sources of electricity and heat that create little or no carbon dioxide. One is **geothermal heat**, which uses heat from inside Earth. **Fuel cells**, which make electricity from air and a fuel (such as natural gas), also produce much less carbon dioxide than just burning the gas. The goal, however, is a fuel cell that runs on **hydrogen** because if the hydrogen is made with renewable sources of electricity, this fuel cell will create no carbon dioxide.

Geothermal heat

The rocks below Earth's crust are so hot they are often **molten**. In some places molten rock, or lava, erupts through cracks in the crust to form **volcanoes**. In other places, Earth's heat provides a constant supply of hot water. Hot springs and **geysers** spout from the ground in Iceland, New Zealand, and California. In Iceland the hot springs are channeled into pipes to provide 90 percent of the hot water used by buildings in and around the capital city of Reykjavik.

But you do not need to have a hot spring to take advantage of Earth's heat. The heat seeps through the solid rocks everywhere, so that the temperature a few feet below the surface is constantly 45 to 70° F (7 to 21 °C). **Heat pumps** can be used to capture this heat, generating extra heat in winter and cooling buildings in the summer.

Steaming hot water escapes through the ground in Iceland. Some of it is diverted into the buildings of the city of Reykjavik.

Fuel cells

A fuel cell is similar to a battery that does not run out and does not need to be recharged. When hydrogen and oxygen are combined in a chemical reaction, they produce water and electricity. In a solid oxide fuel cell, a fuel processor changes a fossil fuel such as natural gas into hydrogen, and the fuel cell then uses the hydrogen to generate electricity and heat. Using natural gas in this way gives much more energy than burning it in a power station. Fuel cells are still expensive, but the price will drop and they will become more common during the next 10 years.

ALL-PURPOSE FUEL
In the future, cars as well as central heating boilers will probably use fuel cells. By about 2050 fuel cells in cars and in buildings will probably work together. At night, when the fuel processor is not needed to feed the building's fuel cell, it could change natural gas to hydrogen to refuel the car. Instead of filling your car with gasoline in the future, you could plug it into an outlet in the outside wall of your home to fill its cylinders with hydrogen.

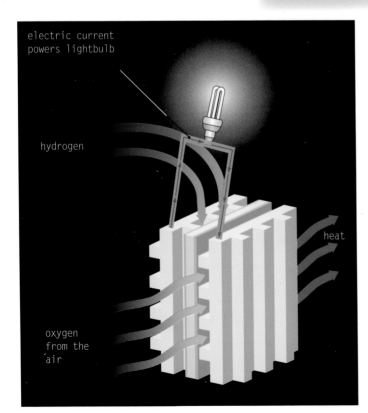

electric current powers lightbulb

hydrogen

heat

oxygen from the air

A fuel cell is like a battery. As hydrogen atoms combine with oxygen atoms, they produce electricity. Unlike a battery, it keeps going as long as it has a continuous supply of fuel.

The Immediate Crisis

Buildings in the future may generate their own electricity from the Sun, wind, and from natural gas and hydrogen fuel cells, but it will take many years before the technology is applied widely. Can people continue as they are and wait for these changes to take effect? The answer is definitely not. Global warming is already happening even faster than scientists originally predicted.

Evidence of global warming

Earth is already experiencing more frequent and more severe storms. Summers are getting hotter and winters are becoming milder. Plants and animals are now growing and living in parts of the world that used to be too cold for them. But the strongest evidence of global warming comes from glaciers Glaciers on high mountains, as well as in the Arctic and Antarctic, are retreating. Glaciers always melt a bit in the summer and refreeze in winter, but now glaciers are melting faster and refreezing less.

Delayed effect

Present global warming is actually caused by carbon dioxide that was emitted several years ago. It takes a while for extra carbon dioxide to cause an increase in temperature, so we know that carbon dioxide we have recently emitted will cause a further rise. Even if we stopped emitting any carbon dioxide now, the temperature of Earth will continue to rise a little due to the extra carbon dioxide already in the atmosphere.

Hurricane Dennis hit Florida in July 2005. Hurricanes damage buildings and threaten people's lives.

Most glaciers are now smaller than they used to be. This is the clearest evidence of global warming. The lake (below) was recently a glacier (above).

Out of control

Scientists define the weight of carbon dioxide in the atmosphere in parts per million (ppm). They analyze the atmosphere and estimate the weight of carbon dioxide in, for example, one million tons of air. During the last century it increased by 31 percent from 280 ppm to 368 ppm. By 2005 it had reached 381 ppm—that is, 381 tons in every million tons—and it is continuing to rise by 6 to 7 ppm per year. Until now, global warming has been mainly caused by humans, but scientists are worried that, as the temperature rises, it will trigger various natural events that will accelerate the process. These events are called **tipping points.**

AN ALTERNATIVE SOLUTION?

One scientist has suggested scattering chemical particles high above the clouds to reflect sunlight back into space and so counteract global warming. He got the idea from the eruption of Mount Pinatubo in 1991. The volcano, which spewed thousands of tons of sulfur high into the air, reduced world temperatures by almost 1 °F (0.5 °C). The plan would be extremely expensive, costing up to $50 billion every two years. It would be much better to spend the money on projects that permanently reduce carbon dioxide.

Tipping points

A tipping point is when the rise in the temperature of the land or sea triggers a natural event that produces a sudden acceleration in global warming. So far the increase in global warming has been caused by human activities and is still within our control. When tipping points begin to kick in, however, people will have to take more drastic action to try to regain control, which might not be possible.

Arctic ice

The Arctic Ocean is covered with a thick, white layer of ice. White is the color that reflects the most light and heat, so most of the sunlight that hits the Arctic Ocean is reflected back into the air and space. As Earth warms up, however, the thick ice that covers this ocean will begin to melt, revealing the dark-colored water below. Dark colors absorb light and heat, so the water will become warmer, melting the rest of the ice at an ever-increasing rate.

The **tundra** is swampy land around the Arctic Ocean that is permanently frozen below the surface. The soil consists of partly decayed plants that have been growing there for millions of years. If Earth warms by 3.6 to 7 °F (2 to 4 °C), this icy ground will begin to melt and billions of tons of the gases carbon dioxide and **methane**, which are stored in the soil, will be released. This will accelerate global warming and further accelerate the thawing of the tundra.

Rain forests

Warmer temperatures are already making the edges of the Amazon **rain forest** drier so that forest fires easily take hold. They may be started by a flash of lightning, but they spread rapidly, destroying many trees that have taken hundreds of years to grow. Rain forests need to be preserved, not just because of their huge number of different kinds of plants and animals, but also because they can lock up large amounts of carbon for hundreds of years.

ADAPT OR CHANGE?

Some argue that people should adapt to climate change. However, the cost of adapting to global warming is many times greater than the cost of changing to low-carbon technologies now.

28

This forest has been set on fire deliberately to clear land for agriculture. Burning forests contributes up to 20 percent of the world's excess carbon emissions.

If the trees burn, they will release billions of tons of carbon dioxide into the air, which will warm Earth further, thus destroying more trees.

A window of opportunity

There is still time to avoid these catastrophes. Scientists predict that it will not be until about 2015 before the first tipping points are triggered. This time must be used to reduce carbon dioxide emissions.

The Thames Barrier was built about 25 years ago to protect London from rising sea levels. It already needs to be made higher. Dealing with the effects of global warming will be more expensive than investing in changes that will prevent it.

Race to Save the Planet

There is not time to sit back and wait for technology to save the planet. We need to act now to reduce the amount of fossil fuel we burn and the amount of carbon dioxide we pump into the atmosphere. We can actually do this quite easily—cutting out waste could save an amazing 30 percent of carbon dioxide emissions. Most buildings leak energy, and the way we live in them wastes even more.

Wasting energy

People in developed countries waste huge amounts of energy. Buildings are overheated in winter and overcooled in summer, and the buildings themselves are often so badly insulated that much of the heating or cooling leaks out. Electric lights may seem insignificant, but they are a huge source of waste. Many people tend to leave them on when they are not needed, and most of the bulbs we use are the wrong kind—a kind that wastes three-quarters of the energy used to light them.

Which uses more energy— turning up the central heating when you are cold or putting on warm clothes?

Preparing for the future

Cutting out waste will not only save carbon dioxide emissions now, but it will also make it easier to introduce new technology. Solar panels and fuel cells generate electricity, but not an unlimited amount. The less electricity used in buildings, the better these innovations will work.

A choice

Something as simple as turning off a light may not make much of a difference, but many small differences add up, and the more people who save energy now, the less carbon dioxide will be produced. It is our future that is at stake. The race against global warming will be won or lost in our lifetime, and the next 10 years are crucial.

This diagram shows how many gigatons of carbon dioxide were produced by these countries in 2002 and how much they might produce in 2025. (1 gigaton is equal to 1 billion tons.)

WHO WILL BE MOST AFFECTED?

The people who will suffer the most from global warming are the majority of the world's population—those who live in poorer, **developing countries**. They are most likely to die of famine, disease, and flooding. But it is people in developed countries who have produced most greenhouses gases. Less than 5 percent of the world's population lives in the United States, but the U.S. has produced 25 percent of the excess carbon dioxide. Great Britain, Australia, and other industrialized countries all produce much more than their fair share of greenhouse gases. So, who should do something about it—people in developed countries or those in developing countries?

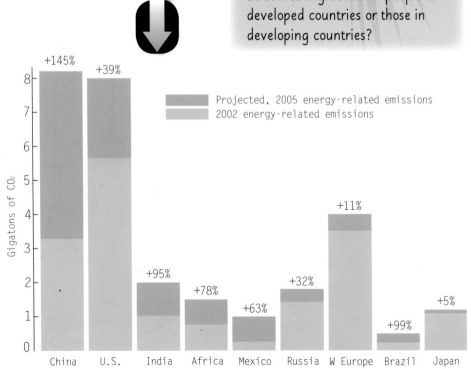

Legend:
- Projected, 2005 energy-related emissions
- 2002 energy-related emissions

Gigatons of CO₂

Country	Percent change
China	+145%
U.S.	+39%
India	+95%
Africa	+78%
Mexico	+63%
Russia	+32%
W Europe	+11%
Brazil	+99%
Japan	+5%

Insulation

Heating and cooling a building uses the most energy, so insulating a home is one of the best ways to save energy. Insulation provides an extra barrier between the inside and outside, so it keeps the inside of a building warmer or cooler than the air outside. Buildings lose most heat through their roofs, walls, windows, and doors. Luckily, both old buildings and new ones can be insulated. In fact, old buildings are likely to be leakier than new ones.

Roofs

More than one-quarter of the heat lost from a house can escape through the roof. To prevent this, the inside of a roof should be covered with a thick layer of insulating material. The most common material is glass fiber (see page 20), but sheep's wool is also a good natural insulator.

This is a heat picture of a typical house. The red areas show where most of the heat is being lost.

Walls

Many houses built in cooler countries since the 1930s have cavity walls. This means that the house has two outside walls with a gap between them. The air in the gap provides some insulation, but it is even better when the gap or cavity is filled with insulating material. When both the walls and roof are insulated, a building needs far less energy to heat it. In summer, it will also stay cooler inside without requiring the air conditioning to be turned so low.

Windows and doors

Heat can easily pass through a single pane of glass. Double glazing loses much less heat. It consists of two panes of glass with a small gap between them. In countries with very cold winters, such as Canada and Scandinavia, windows are often triple glazed with three panes of glass. Double or triple glazing has the advantage that it cuts out noise as well as cold.

Old houses are often drafty. Cold air streams in above and below outer doors, around windows, and even through floors and ceilings. There are many ways to seal gaps, from tape to thin brush strips, to prevent drafts around windows and doors.

Insulating inside a building

Anything that is hotter or cooler than its surroundings will tend to lose or gain heat. Hot water tanks should be well **lagged** with insulating material to keep the heat in. It is better, if possible, to have a freezer in a cool place rather than in a hot kitchen. It will take less energy to keep the inside cool if the outside air is cooler, too.

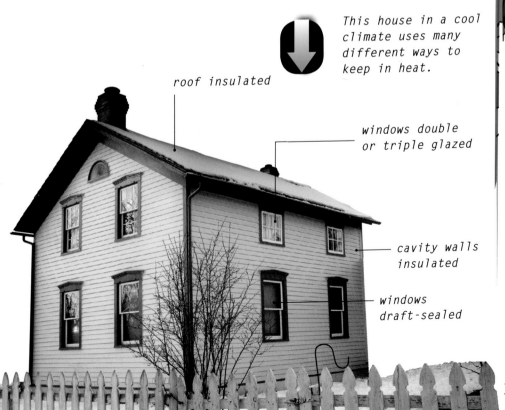

This house in a cool climate uses many different ways to keep in heat.

roof insulated

windows double or triple glazed

cavity walls insulated

windows draft-sealed

Turn down, switch off, and unplug

Many people are very wasteful in the way they use electricity. If electricity comes from a power station that burns fossil fuels, then the more electricity used means that more carbon dioxide is pumped into the air. Even a small change can make a big difference over a year. Electricity is becoming more expensive, so saving it saves money as well.

Turn down the heating

There are several ways you can save energy. Turning down the thermostat on central heating can save up to 10 percent of energy for every 2 °F (1 °C) it is turned down. Turn off radiators in rooms that are not in use, so that the rooms are not heated unnecessarily. And turn down (or turn off) the central heating at night and when everyone is out.

Television screens

When you buy a new television set, buying one with an LCD (liquid crystal display) screen rather than a plasma screen saves energy. This is because plasma screens use more energy.

An LCD screen gives a clear picture and uses less energy than a plasma screen.

Switch off standby

When televisions, DVD players, or CD players are not in use, they should be switched off completely. Machines left on standby can still use about half the amount of electricity they would if they were being used. Why pay money and produce carbon dioxide just to have a small green light on the control panel? Leaving a computer on "sleep" is like leaving it on standby. It is a good idea to put it on sleep if it will not be used for 15 minutes or so, but a computer should be turned off overnight or if it will not be used for several hours.

Batteries

Rechargeable batteries are more efficient than batteries that must be replaced after they run out of energy. Replaceable batteries consume more energy to manufacture and then add to waste when they are finished. Many devices, such as cell phones, digital cameras, MP3 players, and iPods, have rechargeable batteries, but make sure the charger is unplugged after using them. Chargers left plugged in continue to consume electricity.

PATIO HEATERS

Some people heat the air outside their homes! Patio heaters consume large amounts of gas. It has been suggested that the sale of patio heaters and garden lights should be banned.

Patio heaters and garden lights allow people to sit out after dark, but do they use too much energy?

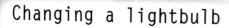

Changing a lightbulb

Electric lighting uses about one-fifth of all the electricity generated. The first electric lightbulbs were invented in 1879 by Thomas Edison in the United States and, independently but at the same time, by Joseph Swan in Great Britain. Most lightbulbs sold today are still the same kind of **incandescent lightbulb**. New long-life, low-energy bulbs, called CFLs and LEDs, use much less energy.

Incandescent lightbulbs

An incandescent lightbulb contains a thin filament inside. When electricity flows through the filament, it glows brightly. The problem is that only about 10 percent of the electricity actually creates light. The other 90 percent is wasted as heat.

Long-life bulbs

CFL stands for **compact fluorescent lamps**. These use about one-fifth as much energy as an incandescent bulb and last over eight times as long. They cost more to buy—although the price is dropping quickly—but they are cheaper overall. They may give a dim light when they are first switched on and take a minute or two to become fully bright. It has been calculated that if every home in the United States changed one incandescent lightbulb to a long-life bulb, it would save the same weight of carbon dioxide emissions as a million cars. Think how much could be saved if all the bulbs in your home were CFLs!

A CFL bulb contains a gas that produces ultraviolet light when electricity passes through it. The white coating on the surface of the bulb changes the ultraviolet light to white light.

LED bulbs

LED stands for **light-emitting diode**. They light up as soon as they are switched on and they can last for decades. The first LED bulbs were colored yellow, green, or red, but white bulbs have since been developed. Small versions of these bulbs are used in clocks and flashlights, and bigger ones are becoming available for rooms.

These cyclists are using LED bulbs in their helmets and on their bicycles. LEDs are much less likely to break than incandescent lightbulbs.

Turn off the light

Most people admit that they leave lights on even when there is no one in the room. At home people could cut electricity bills substantially just by turning off unnecessary lights. Stores and offices are even guiltier. Every room in an office block is often lit all night, although no one is at work. However, long-life bulbs should be left on for 15 minutes before being turned off.

FORCING CHANGE
Australia plans to ban incandescent lightbulbs by 2010, forcing people to switch to long-life bulbs. Should other countries do the same?

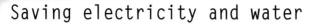

Saving electricity and water

There are many ways to save energy in the kitchen and bathroom. Electricity is about two and a half times as expensive as natural gas for the same amount of energy, so the more natural gas appliances people have, the better. When using appliances, try to waste as little energy as possible. As global warming increases, more areas will suffer from droughts and water shortages, so look for ways of saving water, too.

Refrigerators and freezers

Every time the door of the refrigerator or freezer is opened, warm air is let in. Decide what you want to get out before you open the door! An empty refrigerator or freezer uses more energy to keep it cool than a full one. Keep the refrigerator and freezer well stocked and, if sections become empty, fill them with empty plastic containers or water bottles. The containers stop much of the cold air from escaping when the door is opened.

Instead of using a clothes drier, hang wet clothes outside. They will soon dry.

Washing dishes and clothes

Soak or rinse dirty dishes in cold water instead of using the prewash on the dishwasher, and do not run the dishwasher until it is full. Only wash clothes when they are dirty, and use the most economical setting on the washing machine. Clothes driers take a lot of electricity. Instead of drying wet clothes in a machine, hang them on racks overnight. They will probably be dry by morning. Or try hanging them outside on a sunny day.

Cooking

For small quantities of food, microwave ovens use less energy than conventional ovens. Use the smallest amount of water you need for a cup of coffee and when you are cooking. Pressure cookers and steamers save energy by cooking food faster.

A rain barrel saves water in the garden. Water runs off the roof and collects in the rain barrel.

Saving water

Save water by taking a shower instead of a bath. A bath uses up to 50 gallons (200 liters) of water, whereas a three-minute shower uses only 8 gallons (30 liters). This saves on heating the water. Do not leave the faucet running while brushing your teeth. Rinse your mouth with a glass of water. Also, put a little water in the basin to wash your hands in, instead of running the faucet. Much of the water every home uses is flushed down the toilet. Save water by putting a brick in the toilet cistern so that it holds less water, but be careful not to obstruct the flushing and filling mechanism.

OTHER WAYS OF SAVING WATER

- If you have a garden, collect rainwater in a rain barrel for watering the garden.
- Do not use a sprinkler to water the grass.
- Wash the car using a bucket of water instead of a hose.

Don't be fooled

Some people have come up with a plan that calculates the weight of carbon dioxide your home produces and then asks you to invest in a project that will save the same weight of carbon dioxide elsewhere—often in a village on the other side of the world. Projects include giving away long-life lightbulbs, planting trees, and replacing fossil-fuel stoves with wood-burning stoves. The idea is that by reducing emissions elsewhere, you wipe out your emissions. The plan is called **carbon offsetting**, but does it work?

Calculating emissions

There are several carbon-offsetting companies that have websites on the Internet. To calculate the weight of carbon dioxide produced by your home, you have to type in the amount of money spent on electricity and gas bills over the last year. The websites convert this amount to tons of carbon dioxide. The companies then tell you how much you need to spend to "offset" that weight and offer various projects to choose from.

Planting more trees helps to reduce the amount of carbon dioxide in the air, but everyone should still reduce their carbon emissions.

Does carbon offsetting work?

For carbon offsetting to work, the project that is invested in has to be one that produces a reduction in carbon dioxide. There is often no way of knowing whether that happens. For example, you may pay for free long-life lightbulbs to be given away, but how do you know the people will use them? If you pay for trees to be planted, how many of the trees will actually survive and grow?

For the plan to work, it also has to be one that would not have happened otherwise. There is no saving if you pay for a wind turbine for a village that would have installed the turbine anyway.

Other problems with carbon offsetting

Many carbon-offsetting projects will take many years to save the carbon that you have already created. For example, tree-planting plans often calculate how much carbon dioxide the trees will absorb if they live for 100 years. But the carbon dioxide you have produced is already in the atmosphere.

The biggest problem, however, is that carbon offsetting encourages people to think that they can continue producing carbon dioxide, whereas the reality is that people have to reduce their emissions now. Balancing out an emission with a reduction elsewhere is not enough. People need to both cut emissions and to invest in plans that reduce emissions.

This wood-burning stove replaces a fossil-fuel stove. This is a good project to invest in, but it does not mean that people do not also have to reduce their own carbon dioxide emissions.

The bigger picture

Whatever you can do to reduce your own carbon dioxide emissions is worthwhile, but, on your own, you can only do so much. The more people you can persuade to join you, the better. You could start with your friends and family and then look at buildings in your community. Large buildings, such as your school or city offices, produce much more carbon dioxide than a single home.

Students clean solar panels that heat water for their school, Rishi Valley School, in India.

Ask questions

Think about how your school could save energy. Is it, for example, overheated in winter? If you notice a hot faucet dripping in a bathroom, tell the janitor or whoever is responsible. If you have a school board, ask it to look at ways of saving energy. The board could perhaps raise funds to install solar panels or a wind turbine.

Write to your local government to ask what plans it has in place to save energy in government buildings and what plans it has to reduce future emissions still further. Large companies consume huge amounts of energy. Your home, for example, might produce 50 tons of carbon dioxide a year and your school 2,700 tons, but a large company with many buildings, such as a chain store, could easily produce over 2,700,000 tons. Large companies are very aware of how the public sees them. Writing to them and asking how many tons of carbon dioxide the companies produce and what plans they have to reduce it can be very effective.

Write to politicians

For carbon reductions to work, they have to be made in all industrialized countries. Governments need to work together to agree on how much needs to be saved by each country. Developing countries will need to increase their emissions if they are to improve the standards of living of their people. This means that developed countries must reduce their emissions by more than 80 percent by the year 2050. Write to or email your politicians and ask them whether they support setting international agreements to combat climate change.

CARBON TRADING

Carbon trading is one idea that has been suggested as a way of getting countries to control their carbon emissions. Each country is allocated a weight of carbon that it is allowed to emit. If it exceeds its allocation, it can buy extra allowances from countries that have not used all of their allocations. For this plan to work, the allocations have to be low enough to have an effect. Otherwise, developed countries will simply buy the extra emissions they need and nothing will change. A similar carbon trading plan is already used among some companies in Europe.

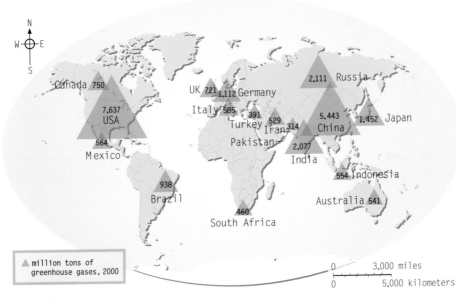

This map shows how different countries contributed to global warming in the year 2000. By 2007 China's emissions equaled those of the United States.

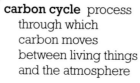

Glossary

carbon cycle process through which carbon moves between living things and the atmosphere

carbon dioxide gas that is found mainly in the atmosphere

carbon off-setting balancing the carbon or carbon dioxide you have produced by paying for a reduction in carbon or carbon dioxide elsewhere

carbon trading system whereby companies and/or countries are each allocated a permitted weight of carbon dioxide they can produce. Those that produce more than their allocation buy extra allowances from companies or countries that produce less than their allocation.

cavity walls outside walls of a building that consist of two walls with a gap, or cavity, between them

climate change change in the usual patterns of climate

compact fluorescent lamp (CFL) lightbulb that makes light when electricity passes through a gas inside it to make it glow. CFLs use less energy and last longer than traditional lightbulbs.

developed country nation, such as the United States or Australia, with a high standard of living due to its advanced economy

developing country nation, such as Kenya or India, where most people rely on farming and are poorer than those in developed nations

drought unusual shortage of rain

emission release of waste substances into the environment, particularly into the atmosphere, rivers, or the sea

fossil fuels coal, oil, and natural gas. These fuels are called fossil fuels because they formed millions of years ago.

fuel cell device that produces electricity by combining the gases hydrogen and oxygen

geothermal heat heat that comes from underground rocks

geyser hot water that spurts from a crack in the ground

glacier large, slow-moving mass of ice in the Arctic, Antarctic, or on high mountains

global warming increase in the average temperature of the surface of Earth

green roof roof that is covered with a layer of soil in which plants grow in order to insulate the building below

greenhouse gases gases in the atmosphere that trap the Sun's heat and so lead to global warming

heat pump device that heats a building by transferring heat from a cooler place to a warmer place. It works like a refrigerator, which also transfers heat from a cooler place (inside the refrigerator) to a warmer place (outside the refrigerator).

hurricane very severe storm involving strong winds over 74 mph (118 kph) and heavy rain

hydrogen one of the gases in the atmosphere. It makes a good fuel.

igloo shelter that Inuits make of blocks of snow

incandescent lightbulb lightbulb that makes light by heating a filament until it glows

insulator material that prevents heat from passing through it

lagged surrounded by insulating material

light-emitting diode device that emits light when an electrical current passes through it

malaria tropical disease that is carried by infected mosquitoes

methane type of natural gas that is one of the greenhouse gases

molten so hot it becomes liquid

mosquito insect that bites and feeds on the blood of animals and people

nomad person who does not live in one place but moves around continually, usually in order to find grazing for sheep, cows, goats, or other animals

passive solar heating using the natural warmth of the Sun to heat a building

photosynthesis process in which carbon dioxide from the air and water is combined using chlorophyll and the energy of sunlight to produce sugar. Photosynthesis mostly takes place in the leaves of green plants and produces oxygen as a waste gas.

photovoltaic panel device that generates electricity using sunlight

power station building or complex of devices that generates large amounts of electricity

quarry pit or cliff face from which stones are blasted or hewn

rain forest forest that grows in warm, wet areas of the world. Most rain forest grows in the tropics and contains millions of different species of plants and animals.

rammed earth mud that has been compacted and dried to make bricks

renewable able to be renewed and is therefore everlasting. Some forms of energy are said to be renewable because they will not run out.

sea level level of the sea halfway between high and low tides

skylight window in roof

solar panel device that uses the heat of the Sun to heat water for a building and uses sunlight to generate electricity. Also known as a photovoltaic panel.

solar pipe device that transmits light through the roof of a building to a lower floor

synthetic material material, such as plastic, nylon, or acrylic, that is made from oil

tipping point critical point in a changing situation that triggers further unavoidable changes

tundra treeless area of land that borders the Arctic and is also found just below the permanent snows of high mountains

typhoon name given to a hurricane in Southeast Asia

volcano place in Earth's crust through which lava sometimes erupts and flows

wind turbine device that uses wind to generate electricity

windcatcher device that pulls fresh, cool air into a building to replace warmer, staler air inside

yurt circular tent used by nomads in Mongolia and Central Asia

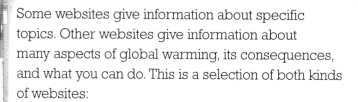

Some websites give information about specific topics. Other websites give information about many aspects of global warming, its consequences, and what you can do. This is a selection of both kinds of websites:

Global warming

www.epa.gov/climatechange/
Website of the U.S. Environmental Protection Agency, which explains global warming and its effect on the environment and ecosystems and suggests various things you can do.

www.wri.org/climate/topic_data_trends.cfm
Website of the World Resources Institute, which gives a world map in which the area of each country is in proportion to the weight of carbon dioxide it emits.

www.energyquest.ca.gov/story/chapter08.html
Energy Quest, a website of the California Energy Commission, explains how coal, oil, and natural gas were formed.

www.commondreams.org/headlines06/0312-03.htm
Gives an article about tipping points in the Arctic and how they will accelerate global warming.

www.climatehotmap.org/
A website that gives a map showing early warning signs of global warming in different continents. Produced by several organizations, including World Resources Institute, Environmental Defense, and World Wildlife Fund.

www.earthinstitute.columbia.edu/crosscutting/climate.html
Website of the Earth Institute at Columbia University in New York City. It outlines the consequences of global warming and suggests some things you can do.

www.greenpeace.org/usa/campaigns/global-warming-and-energy
Website of environmental campaigning organization Greenpeace, with facts and predictions concerning global warming and energy.

www.sierraclub.org/globalwarming/qa/
Website of the Sierra Club, covering global warming and things you can do about it.

www.climatecrisis.net/
Website for the movie *An Inconvenient Truth*, which includes facts about global warming and things you can do.

Solar power

science.nasa.gov/headlines/y2002/solarcells.htm
Websites that shows how a photovoltaic cell works.

A GIANT SUNSHADE IN SPACE

One technological idea for combatting global warming is to build a giant sunshade in space. The sunshade would consist of glass discs that would each reflect a small amount of sunshine. Diverting 2 percent of the Sun's rays is enough to balance global warming, but that would take 16 trillion glass discs placed 1 million miles (1.6 million kilometers) from Earth. It would cost trillions of dollars and could take 30 years to build.

Geothermal power

www.geoexchange.org/about/how.htm

geothermal.marin.org/pwrheat.html
Two websites that explain how geothermal heat works.

Buildings of the future

www.zedfactory.com/bedzed/bedzed.html
Website of the company that designed the Beddington Zero Energy Development, which gives more of their innovative and eco-friendly designs and buildings.

www.earthship.net
Website that gives more information about the Earthship.

Hydrogen fuel

www.hydrogen.co.uk/h2/hydrogen.htm
Gives diagram showing how hydrogen could be produced from renewable sources of electricity and used to power buildings and transportation.

www.fctec.com/fctec_types_pem.asp
Website of the U.S. Department of Defense Fuel Cell Test and Evaluation Center, this tells you about how a hydrogen fuel cell works. The proton exchange membrane fuel cell (PEM) is the best kind of hydrogen fuel cell for buildings.

Carbon offsetting

www.carbonfootprint.com/USA/calculator.html
Website that allows you to calculate how much carbon your family produces.

*I*ndex